DOVER · THRIFT · EDITIONS

Thoreau
A Book of Quotations

HENRY DAVID THOREAU

DOVER PUBLICATIONS, INC.
Mineola, New York

DOVER THRIFT EDITIONS

GENERAL EDITOR: PAUL NEGRI
EDITOR OF THIS VOLUME: BOB BLAISDELL

Copyright

Copyright © 2000 by Dover Publications, Inc.

Bibliographical Note

Thoreau: A Book of Quotations is a new work, first published by Dover Publications, Inc., in 2000.

Library of Congress Cataloging-in-Publication Data

Thoreau, Henry David, 1817–1862.
   Thoreau : a book of quotations / Henry David Thoreau ; [editor of this volume, Bob Blaisdell].
      p. cm. — (Dover thrift editions)
   ISBN 0-486-41428-0 (pbk.)
      1. Thoreau, Henry David, 1817–1862—Quotations. 2. Quotations, American.
I. Blaisdell, Robert. II. Title. III. Series.

PS3042 .B57 2000
818'.302—dc21

00-043165

Manufactured in the United States of America
Dover Publications, Inc., 31 East 2nd Street, Mineola, N.Y. 11501

Note

To COMPILE a collection of Henry David Thoreau's most provocative, compelling, and beautiful statements from a complete edition of his works is akin to snipping off wild-flowers and bringing them indoors and arranging them in a vase. Thoreau once wrote (having overcome his distaste for what could be called "excerpted Nature"): "How fitting to have every day in a vase of water on your table the wild-flowers of the season which are just blossoming!" But what of the swamps and meadows where these flowers were gathered, what of the pesky insects and busy animals and the bracing air, dramatic skies and continuous scenery that set off the flowers to perfect completion? While the context of these five hundred quotations (jostled into seventeen loose-fitting categories) must be imagined, even in their bare, wintry state, they reveal the great American writer's peculiar and resounding mind and his passionate interests in, among many other things, the affairs of politics, pine trees, and painted tortoises.

Though now famous for his "two years, two months, and two days" in his cabin at Walden Pond, Thoreau (1817–1862) lived most of his life in obscurity with his family in Concord, Massachusetts. As a young man he worshiped (and was befriended by) the poet, essayist, and transcendentalist Ralph Waldo Emerson, and for most of his life and long past his death was considered a second-rate imitator of the more famous, less prickly elder man. Thoreau graduated from Harvard in 1837 and, at various times over the next twenty-five years, contributed innovative mechanical improvements to his family's pencil-manufacturing business. For three years he and his brother John ran a school, and taught, among other children, Louisa May Alcott (the school closed with the onset of the fatal illness of John). Thoreau was usually well-liked by children for his candor, playfulness, and informativeness. He became a surveyor and, in spite of his solitariness, quickly became respected and sought after for his scrupulously honest and painstaking work. At the same time, he *was* difficult and antisocial, exasperating friends and acquaintances with his lack of patience with and interest in other people. "I cannot spare my moonlight for the best of man I am likely to get in exchange," he wrote in his journal. He never married nor found himself confessing any strong interest in physical intimacy. He knew himself for an odd fish, and sometimes he saw his devotion to Nature as a choice between It and people—a contest Nature easily won: "I have given myself up to nature; I have lived so many springs and summers and autumns and winters as if I had nothing else to do but live them, and imbibe whatever nutriment they had for me; I have spent a couple of years, for instance, with the flowers chiefly, having none other so binding engagement as to observe when they opened; I could have afforded to spend a whole fall observing the changing tints of the foliage. Ah, how I have thriven on solitude and poverty!"

His journals were his prized possessions and confidants, and their more than three-million words contain the bulk—or at least the seedlings of—all his published work. There is a vitality and enthusiasm in his descriptions of the natural world similar to the exalted utterances of the classical Greek lyric poets in their directness and concision: "Nature now, like an athlete, begins to strip herself in earnest for her contest with her great antagonist Winter. In the bare trees and twigs what a display of muscle!" The wonderful *The Maine Woods* (1864) and the interesting *Cape Cod* (1865) are sparsely represented in this collection not for their lack of attractiveness, but because they are so descriptive and so rarely digressive (his digressions often produce his pithy and poetic pronouncements, or what Emerson called Thoreau's "witty wisdom"). Thoreau reserved his pointed statements for the essays and lectures, the rich hodgepodge called *A Week on the Concord and Merrimack Rivers* (1849), and of course, the classic *Walden* (1854).

When Thoreau's attention was caught by social and moral issues, his rhetoric cut another channel, and his voice echoed the tone of the most volatile and inspiring of New England preachers: "I know this well, that if one thousand, if one hundred, if ten men whom I could name,—if ten honest men only,—aye, if one HONEST man, in this State of Massachusetts, ceasing to hold slaves, were actually to withdraw from this copartnership, and be locked up in the county jail therefor, it would be the abolition of slavery in America. For it matters not how small the beginning may seem to be: what is once well done is done for ever." He is the most popular and, seemingly, least dated of America's nineteenth-century authors, as his voice and attitude often appear thoroughly modern; through his powerful essays on civil disobedience, he in fact exerted great influence on writers and thinkers to come, including Leo Tolstoy, Mahatma Gandhi, and Martin Luther

King, Jr. While his anger at injustice is infectious, so also is his joy in Nature. "I have never got over my surprise," he wrote, "that I should have been born into the most estimable place in all the world, and in the very nick of time, too." When Thoreau died of tuberculosis on May 6, 1862, a friend noted he had "never seen a man dying with so much pleasure and peace."

The quotations come from Dover's *Walden; Or, Life in the Woods* and *Civil Disobedience and Other Essays* and from Bradford Torrey's twenty-volume "Manuscript" edition of Thoreau's *Writings* (Boston, 1906). A new edition of his complete works is being issued by Princeton University Press.

Contents

CONTEMPLATION AND REFLECTION

He is the rich man, and enjoys the fruits of riches, who summer and winter forever can find delight in his own thoughts.

A Week on the Concord and Merrimack Rivers

✧

In all perception of the truth there is a divine ecstasy, an inexpressible delirium of joy, as when a youth embraces his betrothed virgin.

Familiar Letters

✧

New ideas come into this world somewhat like falling meteors, with a flash and an explosion, and perhaps somebody's castle-roof perforated.

Familiar Letters

✧

Genius is a light which makes darkness visible, like the lightning's flash, which perchance shatters the temple of knowledge itself,—and not a taper lighted at the hearth-stone of the race, which pales before the light of common day.

"Walking"

✧

Truth strikes us from behind, and in the dark, as well as from before and in broad daylight.

Journal

✧

Ever and anon something will occur which my philosophy has not dreamed of. The limits of the actual are set some thoughts further off. That which had seemed a rigid wall of vast thickness unexpectedly proves a thin and undulating drapery.

Journal

✧

Objects are concealed from our view, not so much because they are out of the course of our visual ray as because we do not bring our minds and eyes to bear on them, for there is no power to see in the eye itself, any more than in any other jelly.

"Autumnal Tints"

What shall we make of the fact that you have only to stand on your head a moment to be enchanted with the beauty of the landscape?

Journal

✧

It is only necessary to behold thus the least fact or phenomenon, however familiar, from a point a hair's breadth aside from our habitual path or routine, to be overcome, enchanted by its beauty and significance.

Journal

✧

I am, perchance, most and most profitably interested in the things which I already know a little about; a mere and utter novelty is a mere monstrosity to me.   *Journal*

✧

We cannot see anything until we are possessed with the idea of it, take it into our heads,—and then we can hardly see anything else.

"Autumnal Tints"

✧

Whether he sleeps or wakes,—whether he runs or walks,—whether he uses a microscope or a telescope, or his naked eye,—a man never discovers anything, never overtakes anything, or leaves anything behind, but himself.   *Familiar Letters*

✧

This world is but canvass to our imaginations.

A Week on the Concord and Merrimack Rivers

✧

The landscape lies far and fair within, and the deepest thinker is the farthest traveled.   "A Walk to Wachusett"

✧

As Bonaparte sent out his horsemen in the Red Sea on all sides to find shallow water, so I sent forth my mounted thoughts to find deep water.

Familiar Letters

✧

Any sincere thought is irresistible.

A Week on the Concord and Merrimack Rivers

✧

If I am visited by a thought, I chew that cud each successive morning, as long as there is any flavor in it.   *Journal*

Our genius is like a brush which only once in many months is freshly dipped into the paint-pot. It becomes so dry that though we apply it incessantly, it fails to tinge the earth and sky. Applied to the same spot incessantly, it at length imparts no color to it.   *Journal*

❖

It is a far more difficult feat to get up without spilling your morning thought, than that which is often practiced of taking a cup of water from behind your head as you lie on your back and drinking from it.
          Journal

❖

When my thoughts are sensible of change, I love to see and sit on rocks which I have known, and pry into their moss, and see unchangeableness so established.   A *Week on the Concord and Merrimack Rivers*

❖

A man has not seen a thing who has not felt it.   *Journal*

❖

How can we know what we are told merely? Each man can interpret another's experience only by his own.
          A *Week on the Concord and Merrimack Rivers*

❖

No idea is so soaring but it will readily put forth roots.   *Journal*

❖

Like the fruits, when cooler weather and frosts arrive, we too are braced and ripened. When we shift from the shady to the sunny side of the house, and sit there in an extra coat for warmth, our green and leafy and pulpy thoughts acquire color and flavor, and perchance a sweet nuttiness at last, worth your cracking.   *Journal*

❖

When we are unhurried and wise, we perceive that only great and worthy things have any permanent and absolute existence,—that petty fears and petty pleasures are but the shadow of reality.   *Walden*

❖

By a conscious effort of the mind we can stand aloof from actions and their consequences; and all things, good and bad, go by us like a torrent.   *Walden*

❖

None can be an impartial or wise observer of human life but from the vantage ground of what we should call voluntary poverty.   *Walden*

The surface of the earth is soft and impressible by the feet of men; and so with the paths which the mind travels.   *Walden*

❖

The greatest compliment that was ever paid me was when one asked me what I thought, and attended to my answer.

"Life without Principle"

❖

It is a characteristic of wisdom not to do desperate things.   *Walden*

❖

Falsehoods that glare and dazzle are sloped toward us, reflecting full in our faces even the light of the sun. Wait till sunset, or go round them, and the falsity will be apparent.   *Journal*

❖

Great persons are not soon learned, not even their outlines, but they change like the mountains in the horizon as we ride along.   *Journal*

❖

Saw a large hawk circling over a pine wood below me, and screaming, apparently that he might discover his prey by their flight. Travelling ever by wider circles. What a symbol of the thoughts, now soaring, now descending, taking larger and larger circles, or smaller and smaller.

Journal

❖

I believe that the mind can be profaned by the habit of attending to trivial things, so that all our thoughts shall be tinged with triviality.

Journal

❖

Why should pensiveness be akin to sadness? There is a certain fertile sadness which I would not avoid, but rather earnestly seek. It is positively joyful to me.   *Journal*

❖

Man is but the place where I stand, and the prospect hence is infinite. It is not a chamber of mirrors which reflect me. When I reflect, I find that there is other than me.   *Journal*

❖

A higher truth, though only dimly hinted at, thrills us more than a lower expressed.   *Journal*

❖

Each experience reduces itself to a mood of the mind.   *Journal*

DAY AND NIGHT

Rise free from care before the dawn, and seek adventures.   *Walden*

❖

If the sun rises on you slumbering, if you do not hear the morning cock-crow, if you do not witness the blushes of Aurora, if you are not acquainted with Venus as the morning star, what relation have you to wisdom and purity?   *Journal*

❖

Morning is when I am awake and there is a dawn in me.   *Walden*

❖

All memorable events, I should say, transpire in morning time and in a morning atmosphere.   *Walden*

❖

I catch myself philosophizing most abstractedly when first returning to consciousness in the night or morning. I make the truest observations and distinctions then, when the will is yet wholly asleep and the mind works like a machine without friction.   *Journal*

❖

How can one help being an early riser and walker in that season when the birds begin to twitter and sing in the morning?   *Journal*

❖

He who passes over a lake at noon, when the waves run, little imagines its serene and placid beauty at evening, as little as he anticipates his own serenity.   *Journal*

❖

How perfect an invention is glass! There is a fitness in glass windows which reflect the sun morning and evening, windows, the doorways of light, thus reflecting the rays of that luminary with a splendor only second to itself.   *Journal*

❖

Ah, the beauty of this last hour of the day—when a power stills the air and smooths all waters and all minds—that partakes of the light of the day and the stillness of the night!   *Journal*

❖

Unless you watch it, you do not know when the sun goes down. It is like a candle extinguished without smoke.   *Journal*

I thought to-night that I saw glow-worms in the grass, on the side of the hill; was almost certain of it, and tried to lay my hand on them, but found it was the moonlight reflected from (apparently) the fine frost crystals on the withered grass, and they were so fine that they went and came like glow-worms.   *Journal*

❖

The moonlight is rich and somewhat opaque, like cream, but the daylight is thin and blue, like skimmed milk. I am less conscious than in the presence of the sun; my instincts have more influence.   *Journal*

❖

By moonlight we are not of the earth earthy, but we are of the earth spiritual.   *Journal*

EDUCATION

What does education often do? It makes a straight-cut ditch of a free, meandering brook.   *Journal*

❖

The knowledge of an unlearned man is living and luxuriant like a forest, but covered with mosses and lichens and for the most part inaccessible and going to waste; the knowledge of the man of science is like timber collected in yards for public works, which still supports a green sprout here and there, but even this is liable to dry rot.   *Journal*

❖

It is impossible to give the soldier a good education without making him a deserter.   "A Yankee in Canada"

❖

What I was learning in college was chiefly, I think, to express myself, and I see now, that as the old orator prescribed, 1st, action; 2d, action; 3d, action; my teachers should have prescribed to me, 1st, sincerity; 2d, sincerity; 3d, sincerity.   *Familiar Letters*

❖

It is a pleasant fact that you will know no man long, however low in the social scale, however poor, miserable, intemperate, and worthless he may appear to be, a mere burden to society, but you will find at last that there is something which he understands and can do better than any other.   *Journal*

To my astonishment I was informed on leaving college that I had studied navigation!—why, if I had taken one turn down the harbor I should have known more about it.   *Walden*

✧

The student who secures his coveted leisure and retirement by systematically shirking any labor necessary to man obtains but an ignoble and unprofitable leisure, defrauding himself of the experience which alone can make leisure fruitful.   *Walden*

✧

What are the natural features which make a township handsome? A river, with its waterfalls and meadows, a lake, a hill, a cliff or individual rocks, a forest, and ancient trees standing singly. Such things are beautiful; they have a high use which dollars and cents never represent. If the inhabitants of a town were wise, they would seek to preserve these things, though at a considerable expense; for such things educate far more than any hired teachers or preachers, or any at present recognized system of school education.

Journal

✧

We do not learn by inference and deduction and the application of mathematics to philosophy, but by direct intercourse and sympathy.
"Natural History of Massachusetts"

✧

He who cannot read is worse than deaf and blind, is yet but half alive, is still-born.   *Journal*

✧

It is hard to subject ourselves to an influence. It must steal upon us when we expect it not, and its work be all done ere we are aware of it.

Journal

✧

How vain to try to teach youth, or anybody, truths! They can only learn them after their own fashion, and when they get ready.   *Journal*

✧

You must believe that I know before you can tell me.   *Journal*

✧

A man receives only what he is ready to receive, whether physically or intellectually or morally, as animals conceive at certain seasons their kind only. We hear and apprehend only what we already half know.

Journal

It is strange that men are in such haste to get fame as teachers rather than knowledge as learners.   *Journal*

❖

I think that the man of science makes this mistake, and the mass of mankind along with him: that you should coolly give your chief attention to the phenomenon which excites you as something independent of you, and not as it is related to you. The important fact is its effect on me.   *Journal*

❖

The inhumanity of science concerns me, as when I am tempted to kill a rare snake that I may ascertain its species. I feel that this is not the means of acquiring true knowledge.   *Journal*

FREEDOM AND INDIVIDUALISM

As long as possible live free and uncommitted. It makes but little difference whether you are committed to a farm or the county jail.
                                                              Walden

❖

What is it to be free of King George and continue to be the slaves of King Prejudice? What is it to be born free and not to live free?
                                              "Life without Principle"

❖

What is the value of any political freedom, but as a means to moral freedom?   "Life without Principle"

❖

When will the world learn that a million men are of no importance compared with one man?   *Familiar Letters*

❖

I am wont to think that men are not so much the keepers of herds as herds are the keepers of men, the former are so much freer.   *Walden*

FRIENDSHIP AND LOVE

My friend, my friend, I'd speak so frank to thee that thou wouldst pray me to keep back some part, for fear I robbed myself.   *Journal*

Nothing makes the earth seem so spacious as to have friends at a distance; they make the latitudes and longitudes.

Familiar Letters

✧

We are sometimes made aware of a kindness long passed, and realize that there have been times when our friends' thoughts of us were of so pure and lofty a character that they passed over us like the winds of heaven unnoticed; when they treated us not as what we were, but as what we aspired to be.

A Week on the Concord and Merrimack Rivers

✧

A Friend is one who incessantly pays us the compliment of expecting from us all the virtues, and who can appreciate them in us.

A Week on the Concord and Merrimack Rivers

✧

True Friendship can afford true knowledge. It does not depend on darkness and ignorance. A want of discernment cannot be an ingredient in it. If I can see my Friend's virtues more distinctly than another's, his faults too are made more conspicuous by contrast.

A Week on the Concord and Merrimack Rivers

✧

I love my friends very much, but I find that it is of no use to go to see them. I hate them commonly when I am near them. They belie themselves and deny me continually.

Journal

✧

That which we love is so mixed and entangled with that we hate in one another that we are more grieved and disappointed, aye, and estranged from one another, by meeting than by absence.

Journal

✧

I find that I postpone all actual intercourse with my friends to a certain real intercourse which takes place commonly when we are actually at a distance from one another.

Journal

✧

To say that a man is your Friend, means commonly no more than this, that he is not your enemy.

A Week on the Concord and Merrimack Rivers

✧

In human intercourse the tragedy begins, not when there is misunderstanding about words, but when silence is not understood.

A Week on the Concord and Merrimack Rivers

Love is the wind, the tide, the waves, the sunshine. Its power is incalculable; it is many horse-power. It never ceases, it never slacks; it can move the globe without a resting-place; it can warm without fire; it can feed without meat; it can clothe without garments; it can shelter without roof; it can make a paradise within which will dispense with a paradise without.   "Paradise (to Be) Regained"

❖

The heart is forever inexperienced.
                          A Week on the Concord and Merrimack Rivers

❖

In company, that person who alone can understand you you cannot get out of your mind.   *Journal*

❖

If my friend would take a quarter part the pains to show me himself that he does to show me a piece of roast beef, I should feel myself irresistibly invited.   *Journal*

❖

Nothing makes me so dejected as to have met my friends, for they make me doubt if it is possible to have any friends.   *Journal*

❖

I confess that I am lacking a sense, perchance, in this respect, and I derive no pleasure from talking with a young woman half an hour simply because she has regular features.   *Journal*

❖

I have got to that pass with my friend that our words do not pass with each other for what they are worth. We speak in vain; there is no one to hear. He finds fault with me that I walk alone, when I pine for want of a companion; that I commit my thoughts to a diary even on my walks, instead of seeking to share them generously with a friend; curses my practice even. Awful it is to contemplate, I pray that, if I am the cold intellectual skeptic whom he rebukes, his curse may take effect, and wither and dry up those sources of my life, and my journal no longer yield me pleasure nor life.   *Journal*

❖

If I have not succeeded in my friendships, it was because I demanded more of them and did not put up with what I could get; and I got no more partly because I gave so little.   *Journal*

❖

If I am too cold for human friendship, I trust I shall not soon be too cold for natural influences. It appears to be a law that you cannot have a deep sympathy with both man and nature. Those qualities which bring you near to the one estrange you from the other.   *Journal*

HIMSELF

The fact is I am a mystic, a transcendentalist, and a natural philosopher to boot.   *Journal*

❖

May I gird myself to be a hunter of the beautiful, that naught escape me!   *Journal*

❖

Let me forever go in search of myself; never for a moment think that I have found myself; be as a stranger to myself, never a familiar, seeking acquaintance still. May I be to myself as one is to me whom I love, a dear and cherished object.   *Journal*

❖

You may rely on it that you have the best of me in my books, and that I am not worth seeing personally, the stuttering, blundering clod-hopper that I am.   *Familiar Letters*

❖

Methinks I am never quite committed, never wholly the creature of my moods, but always to some extent their critic.   *Familiar Letters*

❖

I trust you realize what an exaggerator I am,—that I lay myself out to exaggerate whenever I have an opportunity,—pile Pelion upon Ossa, to reach heaven so. Expect no trivial truth from me, unless I am on the witness-stand.   *Familiar Letters*

❖

I am still a learner, not a teacher, feeding somewhat omnivorously, browsing both stalk and leaves; but I shall perhaps be enabled to speak with the more precision and authority by and by,—if philosophy and sentiment are not buried under a multitude of details.

Familiar Letters

❖

I love the wild not less than the good.   *Walden*

My imagination, my love and reverence and admiration, my sense of the miraculous, is not so excited by any event as by the remembrance of my youth. *Journal*

✧

In youth, before I lost any of my senses, I can remember that I was all alive, and inhabited my body with inexpressible satisfaction; both its weariness and its refreshment were sweet to me. *Journal*

✧

My body is all sentient. As I go here or there, I am tickled by this or that I come in contact with, as if I touched the wires of a battery. *Journal*

✧

I must confess there is nothing so strange to me as my own body. I love any other piece of nature, almost, better. *Journal*

✧

I have given myself up to nature; I have lived so many springs and summers and autumns and winters as if I had nothing else to do but live them, and imbibe whatever nutriment they had for me; I have spent a couple of years, for instance, with the flowers chiefly, having none other so binding engagement as to observe when they opened; I could have afforded to spend a whole fall observing the changing tints of the foliage. Ah, how I have thriven on solitude and poverty! *Journal*

✧

There was a time when the beauty and the music were all within, and I sat and listened to my thoughts, and there was a song in them. I sat for hours on rocks and wrestled with the melody which possessed me. I sat and listened by the hour to a positive though faint and distant music, not sung by any bird, nor vibrating any earthly harp. *Journal*

✧

How rarely a man's love for nature becomes a ruling principle with him, like a youth's affection for a maiden, but more enduring! All nature is my bride. *Journal*

✧

I cannot spare my moonlight and my mountains for the best of man I am likely to get in exchange. *Journal*

✧

The more thrilling, wonderful, divine objects I behold in a day, the more expanded and immortal I become. *Journal*

Joy and sorrow, success and failure, grandeur and meanness, and indeed most words in the English language do not mean for me what they do for my neighbors.   *Journal*

✧

I love Nature partly because she is not man, but a retreat from him.
                                                                    Journal

✧

I would rather hear a single shrub oak leaf at the end of a wintry glade rustle of its own accord at my approach, than receive a shipload of stars and garters from the strange kings and peoples of the earth.   *Journal*

✧

I have never got over my surprise that I should have been born into the most estimable place in all the world, and in the very nick of time, too.
                                                                    Journal

HUMAN NATURE

We have reason to be grateful for celestial phenomena, for they chiefly answer to the ideal in man. The stars are distant and unobtrusive, but bright and enduring as our fairest and most memorable experiences.
                              A Week on the Concord and Merrimack Rivers

✧

The memory of some past moments is more persuasive than the experience of present ones.   *Familiar Letters*

✧

The prospect of the young is forward and unbounded, mingling the future with the present.   *A Week on the Concord and Merrimack Rivers*

✧

When a man is young and his constitution and body have not acquired firmness, i.e., before he has arrived at middle age, he is not an assured inhabitant of the earth, and his compensation is that he is not quite earthy, there is something peculiarly tender and divine about him.
                                                                    Journal

✧

What old people say you cannot do you try and find that you can.
                                                                    Walden

As difficult to preserve is the tenderness of your nature as the bloom upon a peach.   *Journal*

✧

The youth gets together his materials to build a bridge to the moon, or perchance a palace or temple on the earth, and at length the middle-aged man concludes to build a wood-shed with them.   *Journal*

✧

Such is oftenest the young man's introduction to the forest and wild. He goes thither at first as a hunter and fisher, until at last the naturalist or poet distinguishes that which attracted him and leaves the gun behind.   *Journal*

✧

It is remarkable how long men will believe in the bottomlessness of a pond without taking the trouble to sound it.   *Walden*

✧

No man ever stood the lower in my estimation for having a patch in his clothes; yet I am sure that there is greater anxiety, commonly, to have fashionable, or at least clean and unpatched clothes, than to have a sound conscience.   *Walden*

✧

What I am must make you forget what I wear.   *Journal*

✧

I say, beware of all enterprises that require new clothes, and not rather a new wearer of clothes.   *Walden*

✧

Every generation laughs at the old fashions, but follows religiously the new.   *Walden*

✧

Sincerity is a great but rare virtue, and we pardon to it much complaining, and the betrayal of many weaknesses.   *Familiar Letters*

✧

All men are partially buried in the grave of custom, and of some we see only the crown of the head above ground.
                        A Week on the Concord and Merrimack Rivers

✧

It is very rare that you meet with obstacles in this world, which the humblest man has not faculties to surmount.
                        A Week on the Concord and Merrimack Rivers

However mean your life is, meet it and live it; do not shun it and call it hard names. It is not so bad as you are.

Walden

✧

In the spring I burned over a hundred acres till the earth was sere and black, and by midsummer this space was clad in a fresher and more luxuriant green than the surrounding even. Shall man then despair? Is he not a sprout-land too, after never so many searings and witherings?

Journal

✧

The mass of men lead lives of quiet desperation.   *Walden*

✧

Experience bereaves us of our innocence; wisdom bereaves us of our ignorance.

Journal

✧

We are interested in the phenomena of Nature mainly as children are, or as we are in games of chance. They are more or less exciting. Our appetite for novelty is insatiable. We do not attend to ordinary things, though they are most important, but to extraordinary ones.

Journal

✧

A hard, insensible man whom we liken to a rock is indeed much harder than a rock. From hard, coarse, insensible men with whom I have no sympathy, I go to commune with the rocks, whose hearts are comparatively soft.

Journal

✧

We wonder superfluously when we hear of a somnambulist walking a plank securely,—we have walked a plank all our lives up to this particular string-piece where we are.

A Week on the Concord and Merrimack Rivers

✧

The fault-finder will find faults even in paradise.   *Walden*

✧

Humility like darkness reveals the heavenly lights.   *Walden*

✧

Philanthropy is almost the only virtue which is sufficiently appreciated by mankind. Nay, it is greatly overrated; and it is our selfishness which overrates it.

Walden

Nothing more strikingly betrays the credulity of mankind than medicine. Quakery is a thing universal, and universally successful.
                              A *Week on the Concord and Merrimack Rivers*

❖

It is a very true and expressive phrase, "He looked daggers at me" for the first pattern and prototype of all daggers must have been a glance of the eye.   A *Week on the Concord and Merrimack Rivers*

❖

I am sorry to think that you do not get a man's most effective criticism until you provoke him. Severe truth is expressed with some bitterness.
                                                              Journal

❖

Fame is not just. It never finely or discriminatingly praises, but coarsely hurrahs.   *Journal*

LAW AND GOVERNMENT

That government is best which governs not at all.
                                              "Civil Disobedience"

❖

Wherever a man goes men will pursue and paw him with their dirty institutions.   *Journal*

❖

There will never be a really free and enlightened State, until the State comes to recognize the individual as a higher and independent power, from which all its own power and authority are derived, and treats him accordingly.   "Civil Disobedience"

❖

Under a government which imprisons any unjustly, the true place for a just man is also a prison.   "Civil Disobedience"

❖

The law will never make men free; it is men who have got to make the law free. They are the lovers of law and order, who observe the law when the government breaks it.   "Slavery in Massachusetts"

It is not desirable to cultivate a respect for the law, so much as for the right. The only obligation which I have a right to assume, is to do at any time what I think right.   "Civil Disobedience"

✧

I know this well, that if one thousand, if one hundred, if ten men whom I could name,—if ten honest men only,—aye, if one HONEST man, in this State of Massachusetts, ceasing to hold slaves, were actually to withdraw from this copartnership, and be locked up in the county jail therefor, it would be the abolition of slavery in America. For it matters not how small the beginning may seem to be: what is once well done is done for ever.   "Civil Disobedience"

✧

Let every man make known what kind of government would command his respect, and that will be one step toward obtaining it.
                    "Civil Disobedience"

✧

What is called politics is comparatively something so superficial and in-human, that, practically, I have never fairly recognized that it concerns me at all.   "Life without Principle"

✧

If you aspire to anything better than politics, expect no cooperation from men. They will not further anything good. You must prevail of your own force, as a plant springs and grows by its own vitality.
                    Journal

✧

The character inherent in the American people has done all that has been accomplished; and it would have done somewhat more, if the government had not sometimes got in its way.   "Civil Disobedience"

✧

When a government puts forth its strength on the side of injustice, as ours to maintain Slavery and kill the liberators of the slave, it reveals it-self a merely brute force, or worse, a demoniacal force. It is the head of the Plug Uglies.   "The Plea for Captain John Brown"

✧

The question is not whether you or your grandfather, seventy years ago, did not enter into an agreement to serve the devil, and that service is not accordingly now due; but whether you will not now, for once and at last, serve God,—in spite of your own past recreancy, or that of your ancestor,—by obeying that eternal and only just CONSTITUTION, which He, and not any Jefferson or Adams, has written in your being.

"Slavery in Massachusetts"

❖

Show me a free State, and court truly of justice, and I will fight for them, if need be; but show me Massachusetts, and I refuse her my allegiance, and express contempt for her courts.

"Slavery in Massachusetts"

❖

The fate of the country does not depend on how you vote at the polls— the worst man is as strong as the best at that game; it does not depend on what kind of paper you drop into the ballot-box once a year, but on what kind of man you drop from your chamber into the street every morning.

"Slavery in Massachusetts"

❖

A distinguished clergyman told me that he chose the profession of a clergyman, because it afforded the most leisure for literary pursuits. I would recommend to him the profession of a Governor.

"Slavery in Massachusetts"

❖

I have not read far in the statutes of this Commonwealth. It is not profitable reading. They do not always say what is true; and they do not always mean what they say.

"Slavery in Massachusetts"

❖

The lawyer's truth is not Truth, but consistency, or a consistent expediency. Truth is always in harmony with herself, and is not concerned chiefly to reveal the justice that may consist with wrong-doing.

"Civil Disobedience"

❖

Nations are possessed with an insane ambition to perpetuate the memory of themselves by the amount of hammered stone they leave. What if equal pains were taken to smooth and polish their manners? One piece of good sense would be more memorable than a monument as high as the moon.

Walden

❖

Some circumstantial evidence is very strong, as when you find a trout in the milk.

Journal

LITERATURE AND WRITING

Read the best books first, or you may not have a chance to read them at all.

A Week on the Concord and Merrimack Rivers

❖

It is necessary to find out exactly what books to read on a given subject. Though there may be a thousand books written upon it, it is only important to read three or four; they will contain all that is essential, and a few pages will show which they are.

Journal

❖

As for the sensuality in Whitman's "Leaves of Grass," I do not so much wish that it was not written, as that men and women were so pure that they could read it without harm.   *Journal*

❖

How much more admirable the Bhagvat-Geeta than all the ruins of the East!   *Walden*

❖

. . . what are the classics but the noblest recorded thoughts of man? They are the only oracles which are not decayed, and there are such answers to the most modern inquiry in them as Delphi and Dodona never gave. We might as well omit to study Nature because she is old.

Walden

❖

[Chaucer] is so natural and cheerful, compared with later poets, that we might almost regard him as a personification of spring.

A Week on the Concord and Merrimack Rivers

❖

Reading the classics, or conversing with those old Greeks and Latins in their surviving works, is like walking amid the stars and constellations.

A Week on the Concord and Merrimack Rivers

❖

Thought greets thought over the widest gulfs of time with unerring freemasonry.   *Journal*

❖

Some hard and dry book in a dead language, which you have found it

impossible to read at home, but for which you have still a lingering regard, is the best to carry with you on a journey.
A Week on the Concord and Merrimack Rivers

❖

It is enough if Homer but say the sun sets. He is as serene as nature, and we can hardly detect the enthusiasm of the bard. It is as if nature spoke. . . . Each reader discovers for himself, that, with respect to the simpler features of nature, succeeding poets have done little else than copy his similes.   *A Week on the Concord and Merrimack Rivers*

❖

Ancient history . . . is written as if the spectator should be thinking of the backside of the picture on the wall, or as if the author expected that the dead would be his readers, and wished to detail to them their own experience.   *A Week on the Concord and Merrimack Rivers*

❖

One who has just come from reading perhaps one of the best English books will find how many with whom he can converse about it?
Walden

❖

The poet is he who can write some pure mythology to-day without the aid of posterity.   *A Week on the Concord and Merrimack Rivers*

❖

. . . if men read aright, methinks they would never read anything but poems.   *A Week on the Concord and Merrimack Rivers*

❖

Some books ripple on like a stream, and we feel that the author is in the full tide of discourse.   *Journal*

❖

Whatever book or sentence will bear to be read twice, we may be sure was thought twice.   *Journal*

❖

Genius is the worst of lumber, if the poet would float upon the breeze of popularity.   *A Week on the Concord and Merrimack Rivers*

❖

Everything that is printed and bound in a book contains some echo at least of the best that is in literature.
A Week on the Concord and Merrimack Rivers

Language is the most perfect work of art in the world. The chisel of a thousand years retouches it.   *Journal*

❖

I want nothing better than a good word. The name of a thing may easily be more than the thing itself to me.   "A Yankee in Canada"

❖

What a good word is "flame," expressing the form and soul of fire, lambent with forked tongue!   *Journal*

❖

A written word is the choicest of relics. It is something at once more intimate with us and more universal than any other work of art. It is the work of art nearest to life itself.   *Walden*

❖

Where shall we look for standard English but to the words of any man who has a depth of feeling in him?   *Journal*

❖

His style is eminently colloquial, and no wonder it is strange to meet with in a book. It is not literary or classical; it has not the music of poetry, nor the pomp of philosophy, but the rhythms and cadences of conversation endlessly repeated.   "Thomas Carlyle and His Works"

❖

A work of genius is rough-hewn from the first, because it anticipates the lapse of time, and has an ingrained polish, which still appears when fragments are broken off, an essential quality of its substance.
                    A Week on the Concord and Merrimack Rivers

❖

No man's thoughts are new, but the style of their expression is the never-failing novelty which cheers and refreshes men.
                              "Thomas Carlyle and His Works"

❖

In Literature it is only the wild that attracts us. Dullness is but another name for tameness.   "Walking"

❖

You can't read any genuine history—as that of Herodotus or the Venerable Bede—without perceiving that our interest depends not on the subject but on the man,—on the manner in which he treats the subject and the importance he gives it.   *Journal*

All that interests the reader is the depth and intensity of the life excited.
Journal

✧

Wherever men have lived there is a story to be told, and it depends chiefly on the storyteller or historian whether that is interesting or not.
Journal

✧

Most events recorded in history are more remarkable than important, like eclipses of the sun and moon, by which all are attracted, but whose effects no one takes the trouble to calculate.
A Week on the Concord and Merrimack Rivers

✧

The rarest quality in an epitaph is truth.
A Week on the Concord and Merrimack Rivers

✧

Our books of science, as they improve in accuracy, are in danger of losing the freshness and vigor and readiness to appreciate the real laws of Nature, which is a marked merit in the oft-times false theories of the ancients.   *A Week on the Concord and Merrimack Rivers*

✧

I am constantly assisted by the books in identifying a particular plant and learning some of its humbler uses, but I rarely read a sentence in a botany which reminds me of flowers or living plants. Very few indeed write as if they had seen the thing which they pretend to describe.
Journal

✧

A man's interest in a single bluebird is worth more than a complete but dry list of the fauna and flora of a town.
Familiar Letters

✧

A history of animated nature must itself be animated.   *Journal*

✧

We love eloquence for its own sake, and not for any truth which it may utter, or any heroism it may inspire.
"Civil Disobedience"

✧

The most attractive sentences are, perhaps, not the wisest, but the surest and the roundest. They are spoken firmly and conclusively, as if the speaker had a right to know what he says, and if not wise, they have at least been well learned.

A Week on the Concord and Merrimack Rivers

❖

Our orators might learn much from the Indians. They are remarkable for their precision; nothing is left at loose ends.   *Journal*

❖

Generally, if I can only get the ears of an audience, I do not care whether they say they like my lecture or not.   *Journal*

❖

It takes two to speak the truth,—one to speak, and one to hear.

A Week on the Concord and Merrimack Rivers

❖

Blessed are they who never read a newspaper, for they shall see Nature, and, through her, God.   *Familiar Letters*

❖

I believe that, in this country, the press exerts a greater and a more pernicious influence than the Church did in its worst period.

"Slavery in Massachusetts"

❖

The newspaper is a Bible which we read every morning and every afternoon, standing and sitting, riding and walking. It is a Bible which every man carries in his pocket, which lies on every table and counter, and which the mail, and thousands of missionaries, are continuously dispensing. It is, in short, the only book which America has printed, and which America reads. So wide is its influence.

"Slavery in Massachusetts"

❖

It is surprising what a tissue of trifles and crudities make the daily news. For one event of interest there are nine hundred and ninety-nine insignificant, but about the same stress is laid on the last as on the first.

Journal

❖

To speak critically, I never received more than one or two letters in my life . . . that were worth the postage.   *Walden*

❖

In such a letter as I like there will be the most naked and direct speech, the least circumlocution.   *Journal*

. . . letter-writing too often degenerates into a communicating of facts, and not of truths; of other men's deeds and not our thoughts. What are the convulsions of a planet, compared with the emotions of the soul? or the rising of a thousand suns, if that is not enlightened by a ray?

Familiar Letters

❖

Let me suggest a theme for you: to state to yourself precisely and completely what that walk over the mountains amounted to for you,—returning to this essay again and again, until you are satisfied that all that was important in your experience is in it. *Familiar Letters*

❖

As for style of writing, if one has anything to say, it drops from him simply and directly, as a stone falls to the ground. *Familiar Letters*

❖

When the poetic frenzy seizes us, we run and scratch with our pen, intent only on worms, calling our mates around us, like the cock, and delighting in the dust we make, but do not detect where the jewel lies, which, perhaps, we have in the meantime cast to a distance, or quite covered up again. *A Week on the Concord and Merrimack Rivers*

❖

It is wise to write on many subjects, to try many themes, that so you may find the right and inspiring one. . . . You must try a thousand themes before you find the right one, as nature makes a thousand acorns to get one oak. *Journal*

❖

The more you have thought and written on a given theme, the more you can still write. Thought breeds thought. It grows under your hands. *Journal*

❖

Say the thing with which you labor. It is a waste of time for the writer to use his talents merely. Be faithful to your genius. Write in the strain that interests you most. Consult not the popular taste. *Journal*

❖

Do not speak for other men; speak for yourself. *Journal*

❖

There is no such thing as pure objective observation. Your observations, to be interesting, i.e. to be significant, must be subjective. The sum of what the writer of whatever class has to report is simply some human experience, whether he be poet or philosopher or man of science.   *Journal*

✧

All that a man has to say or do that can possibly concern mankind, is in some shape or other to tell the story of his love,—to sing; and, if he is fortunate and keeps alive, he will be forever in love.   *Journal*

✧

My themes shall not be far-fetched. I will tell of homely every-day phenomena and adventures.   *Journal*

✧

It is surprising how much, from the habit of regarding writing as an accomplishment, is wasted on form.   *Journal*

✧

Essentially your truest poetic sentence is as free and lawless as a lamb's bleat.   *Journal*

✧

. . . unconsidered expressions of our delight which any natural object draws from us are something complete and final in themselves, since all nature is to be regarded as it concerns man; and who knows how near to absolute truth such unconscious affirmations may come?

Journal

✧

There is no more Herculean task than to think a thought about this life and then get it expressed.   *Journal*

✧

A sentence should read as if its author, had he held a plow instead of a pen, could have drawn a furrow deep and straight to the end.
                        A Week on the Concord and Merrimack Rivers

✧

Who cares what a man's style is, so it is intelligible,—as intelligible as his thought. Literally and really, the style is no more than the stylus, the pen he writes with; and it is not worth scraping and polishing, and gilding, unless it will write his thoughts the better for it.
                                    "Thomas Carlyle and His Works"

✧

Never endeavor consciously to supply the tone which you think proper for certain sentences. It is as if a man whose mind was at ease should supply the tones and gestures for a man in distress who found only the words; as when one makes a speech and another behind him makes gestures. *Journal*

✧

I find that I use many words for the sake of emphasis which really add nothing to the force of my sentences, and they look relieved the moment I have cancelled these. *Journal*

✧

In correcting manuscripts, which I do with sufficient phlegm, I find that I invariably turn out much that is good along with the bad, which it is then impossible for me to distinguish—so much for keeping bad company; but after the lapse of time, having purified the main body and thus created a distinct standard for comparison, I can review the rejected sentences and easily detect those which deserve to be readmitted. *Journal*

✧

Methinks the scent is a more primitive inquisition than the eye, more oracular and trustworthy. When I criticise my own writing, I go by the scent, as it were. The scent reveals, of course, what is concealed from the other senses. By it I detect earthiness. *Journal*

✧

It is fatal to the writer to be too much possessed by his thought. Things must lie a little remote to be described. *Journal*

✧

The surliness with which the woodchopper speaks of his woods, handling them as indifferently as his axe, is better than the mealy-mouthed enthusiasm of the lover of Nature.
A Week on the Concord and Merrimack Rivers

✧

The scholar may be sure that he writes the tougher truth for the calluses on his palms. *A Week on the Concord and Merrimack Rivers*

✧

How vain it is to sit down to write when you have not stood up to live! Methinks that the moment my legs begin to move, my thoughts begin to flow, as if I had given vent to the stream at the lower end and consequently new fountains flowed into it at the upper. *Journal*

✧

We cannot write well or truly but what we write with gusto. The body, the senses, must conspire with the mind. Expression is the act of the whole man, that our speech may be vascular. *Journal*

Whatever things I perceive with my entire man, those let me record, and it will be poetry.   *Journal*

✧

It is in vain to write on the seasons unless you have the seasons in you.   *Journal*

✧

Time never passes so quickly and unaccountably as when I am engaged in composition, i.e. in writing down my thoughts. Clocks seem to have been put forward.   *Journal*

✧

My Journal should be the record of my love. I would write in it only of the things I love, my affection for any aspect of the world, what I love to think of.   *Journal*

✧

A journal, a book that shall contain a record of all your joy, your ecstasy.   *Journal*

✧

It is a record of the mellow and ripe moments that I would keep. I would not preserve the husk of life, but the kernel.   *Journal*

✧

It is surprising how any reminiscence of a different season of the year affects us. When I meet with any such in my Journal, it affects me as poetry, and I appreciate that other season and that particular phenomenon more than at the time. The world so seen is all one spring, and full of beauty. You only need to make a faithful record of an average summer day's experience and summer mood, and read it in the winter, and it will carry you back to more than that summer day alone could show.   *Journal*

✧

A journal is a record of experiences and growth, not a preserve of things well done and said.   *Journal*

✧

In a journal it is important in a few words to describe the weather, or character of the day, as if affects our feelings. That which was so important at the time cannot be unimportant to remember.   *Journal*

✧

Of all strange and unaccountable things this journalizing is the strangest. It will allow nothing to be predicated of it; its good is not good, nor its bad bad. If I make a huge effort to expose my innermost and richest wares to light, my counter seems cluttered with the meanest homemade stuffs; but after months or years I may discover the wealth of India, and whatever rarity is brought overland from Cathay, in that confused heap, and what perhaps seemed a festoon of dried apple or pumpkin will prove a string of Brazilian diamonds, or pearls from Coromandel. *Journal*

✧

It is remarkable how suggestive the slightest drawing as a memento of things seen. For a few years past I have been accustomed to make a rude sketch in my journal of plants, ice, and various natural phenomena, and though the fullest accompanying description may fail to recall my experience, these rude outline drawings do not fail to carry me back to that time and scene. It is as if I saw the same thing again, and I may again attempt to describe it in words if I choose. *Journal*

✧

I would fain make two reports in my Journal, first the incidents and observations of to-day; and by to-morrow I review the same and record what was omitted before, which will often be the most significant and poetic part. I do not know at first what it is that charms me. The men and things of to-day are wont to lie fairer and truer in to-morrow's memory. *Journal*

✧

The writer needs the suggestion and correction that a correspondent or companion is. I sometimes remember something which I have told another as worth telling to myself, i.e. writing in my Journal. *Journal*

✧

As travellers go round the world and report natural objects and phenomena, so faithfully let another stay at home and report the phenomena of his own life,—catalogue stars, those thoughts whose orbits are as rarely calculated as comets. *Journal*

✧

Is not the poet bound to write his own biography? Is there any other work for him but a good journal? We do not wish to know his imaginary hero, but how he, the actual hero, lived from day to day. *Journal*

✧

The poet must be continually watching the moods of his mind, as the astronomer watches the aspects of the heavens. *Journal*

The poet is a man who lives at last by watching his moods. An old poet comes at last to watch his moods as narrowly as a cat does a mouse.

Journal

✧

He who cannot exaggerate is not qualified to utter truth. No truth, we think, was ever expressed but with this sort of emphasis, so that for the time there seemed to be no other. Moreover, you must speak loud to those who are hard of hearing, and so you acquire a habit of shouting to those who are not.   "Thomas Carlyle and His Works"

MONEY AND BUSINESS

If a man walk in the woods for love of them half of each day, he is in danger of being regarded as a loafer; but if he spends his whole day as a speculator, shearing off those woods and making earth bald before her time, he is esteemed an industrious and enterprising citizen.

"Life without Principle"

✧

Enjoy the land, but own it not.   *Walden*

✧

The poor rich man! all he has is what he has bought. What I see is mine.   *A Week on the Concord and Merrimack Rivers*

✧

Let me see man a-farming, a-hunting, a-fishing, a-walking,—anything but a-shopping.   *Journal*

✧

Absolutely speaking, the more money, the less virtue; for money comes between a man and his objects, and obtains them for him; and it was certainly no great virtue to obtain it.   "Civil Disobedience"

✧

The ways by which you may get money almost without exception lead downward. To have done anything by which you earned money merely is to have been truly idle or worse.   "Life without Principle"

✧

A grain of gold will gild a great surface, but not so much as a grain of wisdom.   "Life without Principle"

Men's minds run so much on work and money that the mass instantly associate all literary labor with a pecuniary reward. They are mainly curious to know how much money the lecturer or author gets for his work.

Journal

✧

I know many children to whom I would fain make a present on some one of their birthdays, but they are so far gone in the luxury of presents—have such perfect museums of costly ones—that it would absorb my entire earnings for a year to buy them something which would not be beneath their notice. *Journal*

MORALITY AND CONDUCT

Did you ever hear of a man who had striven all his life faithfully and singly toward an object and in no measure obtained it? If a man constantly aspires, is he not elevated? Did ever a man try heroism, magnanimity, truth, sincerity, and find that there was no advantage in them? that it was a vain endeavor?

Familiar Letters

✧

The higher the mountain on which you stand, the less change in the prospect from year to year, from age to age. *Familiar Letters*

✧

As to how to preserve potatoes from rotting, your opinion may change from year to year; but as to how to preserve your soul from rotting, I have nothing to learn, but something to practice.

Familiar Letters

✧

A man's life should be constantly as fresh as this river. It should be the same channel, but a new water every instant.

A Week on the Concord and Merrimack Rivers

✧

Virtue is a bravery so hardy that it deals in what it has no experience in.

Journal

✧

Moral reform is the effort to throw off sleep. *Walden*

No man who acts from a sense of duty ever puts the lesser duty above the greater.   *Familiar Letters*

❖

When the mathematician would solve a difficult problem, he first frees the equation of all incumbrances, and reduces it to its simplest terms. So simplify the problem of life, distinguish the necessary and the real. Probe the earth to see where your main roots run.   *Familiar Letters*

❖

Our life is frittered away by detail. . . . Simplify, simplify.   *Walden*

❖

Simplicity, simplicity, simplicity! I say, let your affairs be as two or three, and not a hundred or a thousand; instead of a million count half a dozen, and keep your accounts on your thumb nail.   *Walden*

❖

Let your capital be simplicity and contentment.   *Journal*

❖

It would be worth the while to ask ourselves weekly, Is our life innocent enough? Do we live inhumanely, toward man or beast, in thought or act? To be serene and successful we must be at one with the universe. The least conscious and needless injury inflicted on any creature is to its extent a suicide. What peace—or life—can a murderer have?

Journal

❖

If I devote myself to other pursuits and contemplations, I must first see, at least, that I do not pursue them sitting upon another man's shoulders. I must get off him first, that he may pursue his contemplations too.   "Civil Disobedience"

❖

A man has not every thing to do, but something; and because he cannot do every thing, it is not necessary that he should do something wrong.   "Civil Disobedience"

❖

Do not be too moral. You may cheat yourself out of much life so. Aim above morality. Be not simply good; be good for something.

Familiar Letters

❖

Pity the man who has a character to support. It is worse than a large family.   *Journal*

Most of the luxuries, and many of the so-called comforts of life, are not only not indispensable, but positive hindrances to the elevation of mankind.   *Walden*

✧

Do not trouble yourself much to get new things, whether clothes or friends.   *Walden*

✧

How often must one feel, as he looks back on his past life, that he has gained a talent but lost a character!   *Journal*

✧

It is possible for a man wholly to disappear and be merged in his manners.   *Journal*

✧

I would not have every man nor every part of a man cultivated, any more than I would have every acre of earth cultivated: part will be tillage, but the greater part will be meadow and forest, not only serving an immediate use, but preparing a mould against a distant future, by the annual decay of the vegetation which it supports.

"Walking"

✧

The conscience really does not, and ought not to, monopolize the whole of our lives, any more than the heart or the head. It is as liable to disease as any other part.

A Week on the Concord and Merrimack Rivers

✧

Circumstances are not rigid and unyielding, but our habits are rigid.

Familiar Letters

✧

It is to be remembered that by good deeds or words you encourage yourself, who always have need to witness or hear them.

Journal

✧

What exercise is to the body, employment is to the mind and morals.

Familiar Letters

✧

Good for the body is the work of the body, good for the soul the work of the soul, and good for either the work of the other.

Journal

The body is the first proselyte the Soul makes. Our life is but the Soul made known by its fruits, the body. The whole duty of man may be expressed in one line,—Make to yourself a perfect body.   *Journal*

✧

I think if I had had the disposal of this soul of man, I should have bestowed it sooner on some antelope of the plains than upon this sickly and sluggish body.   *Journal*

✧

Man is the artificer of his own happiness. Let him beware how he complains of the disposition of circumstances, for it is his own disposition he blames. If this is sour, or that rough, or the other steep, let him think if it be not his work. If his look curdles all hearts, let him not complain of a sour reception; if he hobbles in his gait, let him not grumble at the roughness of the way; if he is weak in the knees, let him not call the hill steep.   *Journal*

✧

Our whole life is startlingly moral. There is never an instant's truce between virtue and vice.   *Walden*

✧

When we are shocked at vice we express a lingering sympathy with it.
                                                                                          Journal

✧

We must walk consciously only part way toward our goal, and then leap in the dark to our success. What we do best or most perfectly is what we have most thoroughly learned by the longest practice, and at length it falls from us without our notice, as a leaf from a tree.   *Journal*

✧

Nothing can be more useful to a man than a determination not to be hurried.   *Journal*

✧

Let not your life be wholly without an object, though it be only to ascertain the flavor of a cranberry, for it will not be only the quality of an insignificant berry that you will have tasted, but the flavor of your life to that extent, and it will be such a sauce as no wealth can buy.
                                                                                          Journal

✧

Nothing is so sure to make itself known as the truth, for what else waits to be known?   *Journal*

Show men unlimited faith as the coin with which you will deal with them, and they will invariably exhibit the best wares they have.

Journal

✧

Our true character silently underlies all our words and actions, as the granite underlies the other strata.   *Journal*

✧

Speech never made man master of men, but the eloquently refraining from it.   *Journal*

✧

The charm of the Indian to me is that he stands free and unconstrained in Nature, is her inhabitant and not her guest, and wears her easily and gracefully.   *Journal*

✧

To how many, perhaps to most, life is barely tolerable, and if it were not for the fear of death or of dying, what a multitude would immediately commit suicide! But let us hear a strain of music, we are at once advertised of a life which no man had told us of, which no preacher preaches.   *Journal*

✧

I cannot but think it nobler, as it is rarer, to appreciate some beauty than to feel much sympathy with misfortune.   *Journal*

✧

It enriches us infinitely to recognize greater qualities than we possess in another.   *Journal*

NATURE

Even the solid globe is permeated by the living law. It is the most living of creatures. No doubt all creatures that live on its surface are but parasites.   *Journal*

✧

The earth has some virtue in it; when seeds are put into it, they germinate; when turtles' eggs, they hatch in due time. Though the mother turtle remained and brooded them, it would still nevertheless be the universal world turtle which, through her, cared for them as now. Thus the earth is the mother of all creatures.   *Journal*

It takes us many years to find out that Nature repeats herself annually. But how perfectly regular and calculable all her phenomena must appear to a mind that has observed her for a thousand years!

Journal

❖

Nature is full of genius, full of the divinity; so that not a snowflake escapes its fashioning hand.   *Journal*

❖

Nature does not cast pearls before swine. There is just as much beauty visible to us in the landscape as we are prepared to appreciate,—not a grain more.

"Autumnal Tints"

❖

I make it my business to extract from Nature whatever nutriment she can furnish me, though at the risk of endless iteration. I milk the sky and the earth.   *Journal*

❖

If you would learn the secrets of Nature, you must practice more humanity than others.   *Journal*

❖

The doctrines of despair, of spiritual or political tyranny or servitude, were never taught by such as shared the serenity of nature.

"Natural History of Massachusetts"

❖

I hate museums; there is nothing so weighs upon my spirits. They are the catacombs of nature. One green bud of spring, one willow catkin, one faint trill from a migrating sparrow would set the world on its legs again. The life that is in a single green weed is of more worth than all this death.

"Life without Principle"

❖

It is remarkable how, as you are leaving a mountain and looking back at it from time to time, it gradually gathers up its slopes and spurs to itself into a regular whole, and makes a new and total impression.

Journal

❖

If there is nothing new on the earth, still the traveller always has a resource in the skies. They are constantly turning a new page to view.

A Week on the Concord and Merrimack Rivers

The gardener can see only the gardener's garden, wherever he goes. The beauty of the earth answers exactly to your demand and appreciation.   *Journal*

✧

The gardener with all his assiduity does not raise such a variety, nor so many successive crops on the same place, as Nature in the very roadside ditches.   *Journal*

✧

Hope and the future for me are not in lawns and cultivated fields, not in towns and cities, but in the impervious and quaking swamps.
                                                              "Walking"

✧

Man cannot afford to be a naturalist, to look at Nature directly, but only with the side of his eye. He must look through and beyond her. To look at her is fatal as to look at the head of Medusa. It turns the man of science to stone.   *Journal*

✧

We soon get through with Nature. She excites an expectation which she cannot satisfy. The merest child which has rambled into a copse-wood dreams of a wilderness so wild and strange and inexhaustible as Nature can never show him.   *Journal*

NATURE

ANIMALS

How long we may have gazed on a particular scenery and think that we have seen and known it, when, at length, some bird or quadruped comes and takes possession of it before our eyes, and imparts to it a wholly new character.   *Journal*

✧

Whatever my own practice may be, I have no doubt that it is a part of the destiny of the human race, in its gradual improvement, to leave off eating animals, as surely as the savage tribes have left off eating each other when they came in contact with the more civilized.   *Walden*

✧

. . . this hunting of the moose merely for the satisfaction of killing him,—not even for the sake of his hide,—without making any extraor-

dinary exertion or running any risk yourself, is too much like going out
by night to some wood-side pasture and shooting your neighbor's
horses.   *The Maine Woods*

✧

How well-behaved are cows! When they approach me reclining in the
shade, from curiosity, or to receive a wisp of grass, or to share the shade,
or to lick the dog held up, like a calf,—though just now they ran at him
to toss him,—they do not obtrude. Their company is acceptable, for
they can endure the longest pause; they have not got to be entertained.
Journal

✧

I look at a young fox at Derby's. You would say from his step and motions that his legs were as elastic as India-rubber,—all springs, ready at
any instant to bound high into the air. Gravity seems not enough to
keep him in contact with the earth. There seems to be a peculiar principle of resiliency constantly operating in him.   *Journal*

✧

I would rather never taste chickens' meat nor hens' eggs than never to
see a hawk sailing through the upper air again.   *Journal*

✧

What a perfectly New England sound is this voice of the crow! If you
stand perfectly still anywhere in the outskirts of the town and listen,
stilling the almost incessant hum of your own personal factory, this is
perhaps the sound which you will be most sure to hear rising above all
sounds of human industry and leading your thoughts to some far bay in
the woods where the crow is venting his disgust.   *Journal*

✧

Birds shoot like twigs. The young are as big as the old when they leave
the nest; have only got to harden and mature.   *Journal*

✧

When the heron takes to flight, what a change in size and appearance!
It is presto change! There go two great undulating wings pinned to-
gether, but the body and neck must have been left behind somewhere.
Journal

✧

The hooting of the owl! That is a sound which my red predecessors
heard here more than a thousand years ago. It rings far and wide, oc-
cupying the spaces rightfully,—grand, primeval, aboriginal sound.
Journal

A partridge goes off from amid the pitch pines. It lifts each wing so high above its back and flaps so low, and withal so rapidly, that they present the appearance of a broad wheel, almost a revolving sphere, as it whirs off like a cannon-ball shot from a gun.   *Journal*

✧

Let a full-grown but young cock stand near you. How full of life he is, from the tip of his bill through his trembling wattles and comb and his bright eye to the extremity of his clean toes! How alert and restless, listening to every sound and watching every motion! How various his notes, from the finest and shrillest alarum as a hawk sails over, surpassing the most accomplished violinist on the short strings, to a hoarse or terrene voice or cluck!   *Journal*

✧

If I were to be a frog hawk for a month I should soon know some things about the frogs.   *Journal*

✧

Frogs are the birds of the night.   *Journal*

✧

A turtle walking is as if a man were to try to walk by sticking his legs and arms merely out the windows.   *Journal*

✧

What animal is more clumsy than the tortoise? If it wishes to get into the brook, it crawls to its edge and then tumbles, lets itself fall, turning a somerset, perhaps, from the bank to the water,—resigns itself to mere gravity, drawing in its head and members.   *Journal*

✧

I am particularly attracted by the motions of the serpent tribe. They make our hands and feet, the wings of the bird, and the fins of the fish seem very superfluous, as if Nature had only indulged her fancy in making them.   "Natural History of Massachusetts"

✧

I have the same objection to killing a snake that I have to the killing of any other animal, yet the most humane man that I know never omits to kill one.   *Journal*

✧

How did these beautiful rainbow tints get into the shell of the fresh-water clam buried in the mud at the bottom of our dark river? Even the sea-bottom tells of the upper skies.   *Journal*

TREES, GRASS, FRUITS, NUTS, AND FLOWERS

If a plant cannot live according to its nature, it dies; and so a man.
"Civil Disobedience"

✧

We can understand the phenomenon of death in the animal better if we first consider it in the order next below us, the vegetable.   *Journal*

✧

It is with the graves of trees as with those of men, — at first an upright stump (for a monument), in course of time a mere mound, and finally, when the corpse has decayed and shrunk, a depression in the soil.
Journal

✧

. . . the pine is no more lumber than man is, and to be made into boards and houses is no more its true and highest use than the truest use of a man is to be cut down and made into manure.
The Maine Woods

✧

The pine is one of the richest of trees to my eye. It stands like a great moss, a luxuriant mildew, — the pumpkin pine, — which the earth produces without effort.   *Journal*

✧

May I ever be in as good spirits as a willow! How tenacious of life! How withy! How soon it gets over its hurts! They never despair.   *Journal*

✧

Let us have willows for spring, elms for summer, maples and walnuts and tupeloes for autumn, evergreens for winter, and oaks for all seasons. What is a gallery in a house to a gallery in the streets, which every market-man rides through, whether he will or not?   *"Autumnal Tints"*

✧

It is easier to recover the history of the trees which stood here a century or more ago than it is to recover the history of the men who walked beneath them.   *Journal*

✧

Each stick I deal with has a history, and I read it as I am handling it, and, last of all, I remember my adventures in getting it, while it is burning in the winter evening. That is the most interesting part of its history.
Journal

The tree whose fruit we would obtain should not be too rudely shaken even. It is not a time of distress, when a little haste and violence even might be pardoned. It is worse than boorish, it is criminal, to inflict an unnecessary injury on the tree that feeds or shadows us.   *Journal*

✧

If you would make acquaintance with the ferns you must forget your botany. You must get rid of what is commonly called knowledge of them. Not a single scientific term or distinction is the least to the purpose, for you would fain perceive something, and you must approach the object totally unprejudiced. You must be aware that no thing is what you have taken it to be.   *Journal*

✧

A single gentle rain makes the grass many shades greener. So our prospects brighten on the influx of better thoughts.   *Walden*

✧

I sympathize with weeds perhaps more than with the crop they choke, they express so much vigor. They are the truer crop which the earth more willingly bears.   *Journal*

✧

What can be handsomer, wear better to the eye, than the color of the acorn, like the leaves on which they fall polished, or varnished? To find that acorns are edible,—it is a greater addition to one's stock of life than would be imagined. I should be at least equally pleased if I were to find that the grass tasted sweet and nutritious.   *Journal*

✧

The bitter-sweet of a white oak acorn which you nibble in a bleak November walk over the tawny earth is more to me than a slice of imported pineapple.   *Journal*

✧

The great green acorns in broad, shallow cups. How attractive these forms! No wonder they are imitated on pumps, fence and bed posts.   *Journal*

✧

Peaches are unquestionably a very beautiful and palatable fruit, but the gathering of them for the market is not nearly so interesting as the gathering of huckleberries for your own use.   *Journal*

✧

Pears, it is truly said, are less poetic than apples. They have neither the beauty nor the fragrance of apples, but their excellence is in their flavor, which speaks to a grosser sense.   *Journal*

✧

Painters are wont, in their pictures of Paradise, to strew the ground too thickly with flowers. There should be moderation in all things. Though we love flowers, we do not want them so thick under our feet that we cannot walk without treading on them.   *Journal*

✧

How fitting to have every day in a vase of water on your table the wild-flowers of the season which are just blossoming!

Journal

✧

It chanced the other day that I secured a white water-lily, and a season I had waited for had arrived. It is an emblem of purity. It bursts up so pure and fair to the eye, and so sweet to the scent, as if to show us what purity and sweetness reside in, and can be extracted from, the slime and muck of earth.   "Slavery in Massachusetts"

✧

I know of no object more unsightly to a careless glance than an empty thistle-head, yet, if you examine it closely, it may remind you of the silk-lined cradle in which a prince was rocked.   *Journal*

WATER

We are slow to realize water,—the beauty and magic of it. It is interestingly strange to us forever. Immortal water, alive even in the superficies, restlessly heaving now and tossing me and my boat, and sparkling with life!   *Journal*

✧

The ocean is a wilderness reaching round the globe, wilder than a Bengal jungle, and fuller of monsters, washing the very wharves of our cities and the gardens of our sea-side residences. Serpents, bears, hyenas, tigers, rapidly vanish as civilization advances, but the most populous and civilized city cannot scare a shark far from its wharves.

Cape Cod

✧

Creeping along the endless beach amid the sun-squall and the foam, it occurs to us that we, too, are the product of sea-slime.   *Cape Cod*

The finest workers in stone are not copper or steel tools, but the gentle touches of air and water working at their leisure with a liberal allowance of time.

A Week on the Concord and Merrimack Rivers

✧

Water is a pioneer which the settler follows, taking advantage of its improvements.   *The Maine Woods*

✧

What an engineer this water is! It comes with its unerring level, and reveals all the inequalities of the meadow.   *Journal*

✧

. . . in the course of ages the rivers wriggle in their beds, till it feels comfortable under them. Time is cheap and rather insignificant. It matters not whether it is a river which changes from side to side in a geological period or an eel that wriggles past in an instant.

Journal

✧

Other roads do some violence to Nature, and bring the traveller to stare at her, but the river steals into the scenery it traverses without intrusion, silently creating and adoring it, and is as free to come and go as the zephyr.   *A Week on the Concord and Merrimack Rivers*

✧

Water is so much more fine and sensitive an element than earth. A single boatman passing up or down the whole of a wide river, and disturbs its every reflection. The air is an element which our voices shake still further than our oars the water.

Journal

✧

There is something in the scenery of a broad river equivalent to culture and civilization. Its channel conducts our thoughts as well as bodies to classic and famous ports, and allies us to all that is fair and great.

Journal

✧

A lake is the landscape's most beautiful and expressive feature. It is earth's eye; looking into which the beholder measures the depth of his own nature.   *Walden*

✧

The largest pond is as sensitive to atmospheric changes as the globule of mercury in its tube.   *Walden*

It is remarkable how large a mansion of the air you can explore with your ears in the still morning by the waterside.

Journal

RELIGION

Man is as singular as God. *Journal*

✧

We are wont foolishly to think that the creed which a man professes is more significant than the fact he is. *Journal*

✧

The New Testament is remarkable for its pure morality; the best of the Hindoo Scripture, for its pure intellectuality.

A Week on the Concord and Merrimack Rivers

✧

The book has never been written which is to be accepted without any allowance. *A Week on the Concord and Merrimack Rivers*

✧

That nation is not Christian where the principles of humanity do not prevail, but the prejudices of race. *Journal*

✧

What do ye want to hear, ye puling infants? A trumpet-sound that would train you up to mankind, or a nurse's lullaby? The preachers and the lecturers deal with men of straw, as they are men of straw themselves. Why, a free-spoken man, of sound lungs, cannot draw a long breath without causing your rotten institutions to come toppling down by the vacuum he makes. Your church is a baby-house made of blocks, and so of the state. *Journal*

✧

The church is a sort of hospital for men's souls, and as full of quackery as the hospital for their bodies.

A Week on the Concord and Merrimack Rivers

✧

The modern Christian is a man who has consented to say all the prayers in the liturgy, provided you will let him go straight to bed and sleep quietly afterward. "The Plea for Captain John Brown"

We check and repress the divinity that stirs within us, to fall down and worship the divinity that is dead without us.   *Journal*

✧

There is more religion in men's science than there is science in their religion.   *A Week on the Concord and Merrimack Rivers*

SEASONS

Each season is but an infinitesimal point. It no sooner comes than it is gone. It has no duration. It simply gives a tone and hue to my thought.   *Journal*

✧

Spring is brown; summer, green; autumn, yellow; winter, white; November, gray.   *Journal*

✧

No one, to my knowledge, has observed the minute differences in the seasons. Hardly two nights are alike. The rocks do not feel warm to-night, for the air is warmest; nor does the sand particularly. A book of the seasons, each page of which should be written in its own season and out-of-doors, or in its own locality wherever it may be.   *Journal*

✧

We discover a new world every time that we see the earth again after it has been covered for a season with snow.   *Journal*

✧

How silent are the footsteps of Spring!   *Journal*

✧

Now, when the sap of the trees is probably beginning to flow, the sap of the earth, the river, overflows and bursts its icy fetters.   *Journal*

✧

Each new year is a surprise to us. We find that we had virtually forgotten the note of each bird, and when we hear it again it is remembered like a dream, reminding us of a previous state of existence.   *Journal*

✧

How rapidly the young twigs shoot—the herbs, trees, shrubs no sooner leaf out than they shoot forward surprisingly, as if they had acquired a head by being repressed so long. . . . Many do most of their growing for the year in a week or two at this season. They shoot—they spring—and the rest of the year they harden and mature, and perhaps have a second spring in the latter part of summer or in the fall.   *Journal*

✧

As every season seems best to us in its turn, so the coming in of spring is like the creation of Cosmos out of Chaos and the realization of the Golden Age.   *Walden*

✧

I take infinite pains to know all the phenomena of the spring, for instance, thinking that I have here the entire poem, and then, to my chagrin, I hear that it is but an imperfect copy that I possess and have read, that my ancestors have torn out many of the first leaves and grandest passages, and mutilated it in many places.   *Journal*

✧

Not till June can the grass be said to be waving in the fields. When the frogs dream, and the grass waves, and the buttercups toss their heads, and the heat disposes to bathe in the ponds and streams, then is summer begun.   *Journal*

✧

It is dry, hazy June weather. We are more of the earth, farther from heaven, these days.   *Journal*

✧

No summer day is so beautiful as the fairest spring and fall days.

Journal

✧

How much of the year is spring and fall! how little can be called summer! The grass is no sooner grown than it begins to wither.   *Journal*

✧

There is a light on the earth and leaves, as if they were burnished. It is the glistening autumnal side of summer. I feel a cool vein in the breeze, which braces my thought, and I pass with pleasure over sheltered and sunny portions of the sand where the summer's heat is undiminished, and I realize what a friend I am losing.   *Journal*

✧

As I make my way amid rank weeds still wet with the dew, the air filled with a decaying musty scent and the z-ing of small locusts, I hear the distant sound of a flail, and thoughts of autumn occupy my mind, and the memory of past years.   *Journal*

How ever unexpected are these later flowers! You thought that Nature had about wound up her affairs. You had seen what she could do this year, and had not noticed a few weeds by the roadside, or mistook them for the remains of summer flowers now hastening to their fall; you thought you knew every twig and leaf by the roadside, and nothing more was to be looked for there; and now, to your surprise, these ditches are crowded with millions of little stars.   *Journal*

✧

. . . Nature, who is superior to all styles and ages, is now, with pensive face, composing her poem Autumn, with which no work of man will bear to be compared.

A Week on the Concord and Merrimack Rivers

✧

I was just thinking it would be fine to get a specimen leaf from each changing tree and shrub and plant in autumn, in September and October, when it had got its brightest characteristic color, the intermediate ripeness in its transition from the green to the russet or brown state, outline and copy its color exactly with paint in a book,—a book which should be a memorial of October, be entitled October Hues or Autumnal Tints.   *Journal*

✧

Think how much the eyes of painters of all kinds, and of manufacturers of cloth and paper, and paper-stainers, and countless others, are to be educated by these autumnal colors. The stationer's envelopes may be of very various tints, yet not so various as those of the leaves of a single tree.   "Autumnal Tints"

✧

I do not see why, since America and her autumn woods have been discovered, our leaves should not compete with the precious stones in giving names to colors; and, indeed, I believe that in course of time the names of some of our trees and shrubs, as well as flowers, will get into our popular chromatic nomenclature.   "Autumnal Tints"

✧

October is the month for painted leaves. Their rich glow now flashes round the world. As fruits and leaves and the day itself acquire a bright tint just before they fall, so the year near its setting. October is its sunset sky; November the later twilight.   "Autumnal Tints"

✧

It is pleasant to walk over the beds of these fresh, crisp, and rustling leaves. How beautifully they go to their graves! how gently lay themselves down and turn to mould!—painted of a thousand hues, and fit to make the beds of the living. So they troop to their last resting-place, light and frisky. "Autumnal Tints"

❖

As I go through the woods now, so many oak and other leaves have fallen the rustling noise somewhat disturbs my musing. *Journal*

❖

When the leaves fall, the whole earth is a cemetery pleasant to walk in. I love to wander and muse over them in their graves. Here are no lying nor vain epitaphs. "Autumnal Tints"

❖

There are two seasons when the leaves are in their glory, their green and perfect youth in June and this their ripe old age. *Journal*

❖

How much beauty in decay! I pick up a white oak leaf, dry and stiff, but yet mingled red and green, October-like, whose pulpy part some insect has eaten beneath, exposing the delicate network of its veins.

Journal

❖

October answers to that period in the life of man when he is no longer dependent on his transient moods, when all his experience ripens into wisdom, but every root, branch, leaf of him glows with maturity. What he has been and done in his spring and summer appears. He bears his fruit. *Journal*

❖

The season of flowers or of promise may be said to be over, and now is the season of fruits; but where is our fruit? The night of the year is approaching. What have we done with our talent? All nature prompts and reproves us. How early in the year it begins to be late! *Journal*

❖

As the afternoons grow shorter, and the early evening drives us home to complete our chores, we are reminded of the shortness of life, and become more pensive, at least in this twilight of the year. We are prompted to make haste and finish our work before the night comes.

Journal

❖

This is the month of nuts and nutty thoughts,—that November whose name sounds so bleak and cheerless. Perhaps its harvest of thought is worth more than all the other crops of the year. *Journal*

Nature now, like an athlete, begins to strip herself in earnest for her contest with her great antagonist Winter. In the bare trees and twigs what a display of muscle!

Journal

✧

It is now fairly winter. We have passed the line, have put the autumn behind us, have forgotten what these withered herbs that rise above the snow here and there are, what flowers they ever bore.

Journal

✧

If the race had never lived through a winter, what would they think was coming? *Journal*

✧

Now a man will eat his heart, if ever, now while the earth is bare, barren and cheerless, and we have the coldness of winter without the variety of ice and snow; but methinks the variety and compensation are in the stars now. How bright they are now by contrast with the dark earth! *Journal*

✧

How few are aware that in winter, when the earth is covered with snow and ice, . . . the sunset is double. The winter is coming when I shall walk the sky. *Journal*

✧

Imagine the innumerable twigs and boughs of the forest (as you stand in its still midst), crossing each other at every conceivable angle on every side from the ground to thirty feet in height, with each its zigzag wall of snow four or five inches high, so innumerable at different distances one behind another that they completely close up the view like a loose-woven downy screen, into which, however, stooping and winding, you ceaselessly advance. *Journal*

✧

It is for man the seasons and all their fruits exist. The winter was made to concentrate and harden and mature the kernel of his brain, to give tone and firmness and consistency to his thought. Then is the great harvest of the year, the harvest of thought.

Journal

✧

After December all weather that is not wintry is springlike.

Journal

Is not January the hardest month to get through? When you have weathered that, you get into the gulf-stream of winter, nearer the shores of spring. *Journal*

❖

To make a perfect winter day like this, you must have a clear, sparkling air, with a sheen from the snow, sufficient cold, little or no wind; and the warmth must come directly from the sun.

Journal

❖

When the snow is falling thick and fast, the flakes nearest you seem to be driving straight to the ground, while the more distant seem to float in the air in a quivering bank, like feathers, or like birds at play, and not as if sent on any errand. So, at a little distance, all the works of Nature proceed with sport and frolic. *Journal*

❖

The winters come now as fast as snowflakes. It is wonderful that old men do not lose their reckoning. It was summer, and now again it is winter. Nature loves this rhyme so well that she never tires of repeating it. *Journal*

❖

At the end of winter, when the fields are bare and there is nothing to relieve the monotony of the withered vegetation, our life seems reduced to its lowest terms. But let a bluebird come and warble over them, and what a change! *Journal*

❖

In cold weather you see not only men's beards and the hair about the muzzles of oxen whitened with their frozen breath, but countless holes in the banks, which are the nostrils of the earth, white with the frozen earth's breath. *Journal*

❖

How different the sunlight over thawing snow from the same over dry, frozen snow! The former excites me strangely, and I experience a springlike melting in my thoughts. *Journal*

❖

Perhaps what most moves us in winter is some reminiscence of far-off summer. How we leap by the side of the open brooks! What beauty in the running brooks! What life! What society! The cold is merely superficial; it is summer still at the core, far, far within.

Journal

SOLITUDE

I never found the companion that was so companionable as solitude.

Walden

❖

By my intimacy with nature I find myself withdrawn from man. My interest in the sun and the moon, in the morning and the evening, compels me to solitude.   *Journal*

❖

I thrive best on solitude. If I have had a companion only one day in a week, unless it were one or two I could name, I find that the value of the week to me has been seriously affected. It dissipates my days, and often it takes me another week to get over it.   *Journal*

❖

I feel the necessity of deepening the stream of my life: I must cultivate privacy. It is very dissipating to be with people too much.   *Journal*

❖

I do not know if I am singular when I say that I believe there is no man with whom I can associate who will not, comparatively speaking, spoil my afternoon.   *Journal*

❖

Not till we are lost, in other words, not till we have lost the world, do we begin to find ourselves, and realize where we are and the infinite extent of our relations.   *Walden*

❖

Silence is the universal refuge, the sequel to all dull discourses and all foolish acts, a balm to our every chagrin, as welcome after satiety as after disappointment; that background which the painter may not daub, be he master or bungler, and which, however awkward a figure we may have made in the foreground, remains ever our inviolable asylum, where no indignity can assail, no personality disturb us.

A Week on the Concord and Merrimack Rivers

❖

The man I meet with is not often so instructive as the silence he breaks.

Journal

❖

I am tired of frivolous society, in which silence is forever the most natural and the best manners. I would fain walk on the deep waters, but my companions will only walk on shallows and puddles. *Journal*

Why will you waste so many regards on me, and not know what to think of my silence? Infer from it what you might from the silence of a dense pine wood. It is its natural condition, except when the winds blow, and the jays scream, and the chickadee winds up his clock. My silence is just as inhuman as that, and no more. *Familiar Letters*

You think that I am impoverishing myself by withdrawing from men, but in my solitude I have woven for myself a silken web or chrysalis, and, nymph-like, shall ere long burst forth a more perfect creature, fitted for a higher society. *Journal*

TRAVEL

A traveller! I love his title. A traveller is to be reverenced as such. His profession is the best symbol of our life. Going from ___ toward ___; it is the history of every one of us. *Journal*

The question is not where did the traveller go? what places did he see? — it would be difficult to choose between places — but who was the traveller? how did he travel? how genuine an experience did he get? For travelling is, in the main, like as if you stayed at home, and then the question is how do you live and conduct yourself at home? *Journal*

A warm, dripping rain, heard on one's umbrella as on a snug roof, and on the leaves without, suggests comfort. We go abroad with a slow but sure contentment, like turtles under their shells. *Journal*

Simply to see to a distant horizon through a clear air, — the fine outline of a distant hill or a blue mountain-top through some new vista, — this is wealth enough for one afternoon. *Journal*

It is worth the while to walk in wet weather; the earth and leaves are strewn with pearls. What you can recall of a walk on the second day will differ from what you remember on the first day, as the mountain

chain differs in appearance, looking back the next day, from the aspect
it wore when you were at its base, or generally, as any view changes to
one who is journeying amid mountains when he has increased the distance.   *Journal*

✧

I have learned that the swiftest traveller is he that goes afoot.
                                                              Walden

✧

When the spring stirs my blood/With the instinct to travel,/I can get
enough gravel/On the Old Marlborough Road.
                                                            "Walking"

✧

In our most trivial walks, we are constantly, though unconsciously,
steering like pilots by certain well-known beacons and head-lands, and
if we go beyond our usual course we still carry in our minds the bear-
ing of some neighboring cape; and not till we are completely lost, or
turned round,—for a man needs only to be turned round once with his
eyes shut in this world to be lost,—do we appreciate the vastness and
strangeness of Nature.   *Walden*

✧

What business have I in the woods, if I am thinking of something out
of the woods?   "Walking"

✧

Man and his affairs, church and state and school, trade and commerce,
and manufactures and agriculture, even politics, the most alarming of
them all,—I am pleased to see how little space they occupy in the landscape.   "Walking"

✧

How little there is on an ordinary map! How little, I mean, that concerns the walker and the lover of nature. Between those lines indicat-
ing roads is a plain blank space in the form of a square or triangle or
polygon or segment of a circle, and there is naught to distinguish this
from another area of similar size and form.   *Journal*

✧

A man's health requires as many acres of meadow to his prospect as his
farm does loads of muck.   "Walking"

✧

You cannot walk too early in new-fallen snow to get the sense of purity,
novelty, and unexploredness.   *Journal*

Often, I would rather undertake to shoulder a barrel of pork and carry it a mile than take into my company a man. It would not be so heavy a weight upon my mind. I could put it down and only feel my back ache for it.   *Journal*

✧

I come to my solitary woodland walk as the homesick go home.

Journal

✧

This stillness, solitude, wildness of nature is a kind of thoroughwort, or boneset, to my intellect. This is what I go out to seek. It is as if I always met in those places some grand, serene, immortal, infinitely encouraging, though invisible, companion, and walked with him.

Journal

✧

I have walked, perhaps, a particular wild path along some swamp-side all summer, and thought to myself, I am the only villager that ever comes here. But I go out shortly after the first snow has fallen, and lo, here is the track of a sportsman and his dog in my secluded path, and probably he preceded me in the summer as well. Yet my hour is not his, and I may never meet him!   *Journal*

✧

. . . the man who goes alone can start to day; but he who travels with another must wait till that other is ready, and it may be a long time before they get off.   *Walden*

✧

Honest traveling is about as dirty work as you can do, and a man needs a pair of overalls for it.   "A Yankee in Canada"

✧

The perfection of traveling is to travel without baggage. After considerable reflection and experience, I have concluded that the best bag for the foot-traveler is made with a handkerchief, or, if he study appearances, a piece of stiff brown paper, well tied up, with a fresh piece within to put outside when the first is torn.   "A Yankee in Canada"

✧

The walker and naturalist does not wear a hat, or a shoe, or a coat, to be looked at, but for other uses.   *Journal*

✧

Better moccasins, or sandals, or even bare feet, than a tight shoe.

Journal

How many things concur to keep a man at home, to prevent his yielding to his inclination to wander! If I would extend my walk a hundred miles, I must carry a tent on my back for shelter at night or in the rain, or at least I must carry a thick coat to be prepared for a change in the weather.	*Journal*

✧

It is surprising with what impunity and comfort one who has always lain in a warm bed in a close apartment, and studiously avoided drafts of air, can lie down on the ground without a shelter, roll himself in a blanket, and sleep before a fire, in a frosty, autumn night, just after a long rain-storm, and even come soon to enjoy and value the fresh air.	*The Maine Woods*

✧

Most of us are still related to our native fields as the navigator to undiscovered islands in the sea. We can any autumn discover a new fruit there which will surprise us by its beauty or sweetness. So long as I saw one or two kinds of berries in my walks whose names I did not know, the proportion of the unknown seemed indefinitely if not infinitely great.	*Journal*

✧

I think more of skates than of the horse or locomotive as annihilators of distance, for while I am getting along with the speed of the horse, I have at the same time the satisfaction of the horse and his rider, and far more adventure and variety than if I were riding.	*Journal*

✧

What's the need of visiting far-off mountains and bogs, if a half-hour's walk will carry me into such wildness and novelty.	*Journal*

✧

It is in vain to dream of a wildness distant from ourselves.	*Journal*

✧

It matters not where or how far you travel,—the farther commonly the worse,—but how much alive you are.	*Journal*

✧

Is not each withered leaf that I see in my walks something which I have traveled to find?—traveled, who can tell how far? What a fool he must be who thinks that his El Dorado is anywhere but where he lives!	*Familiar Letters*

✧

It is an important epoch when a man who has always lived on the east side of a mountain and seen it in the west, travels round and sees it in the east. Yet the universe is a sphere whose centre is wherever there is intelligence. The sun is not so central as a man.

A Week on the Concord and Merrimack Rivers

✧

When I see only the roof of a house above the woods and do not know whose it is, I presume that one of the worthies of the world dwells beneath it, and for a season I am exhilarated at the thought.

Journal

✧

To go to sea! Why, it is to have the experience of Noah,—to realize the deluge. Every vessel is an ark.   *Cape Cod*

✧

When we have returned from the seaside, we sometimes ask ourselves why we did not spend more time gazing at the sea; but very soon the traveller does not look at the sea more than at the heavens.

Cape Cod

✧

Sailing is much like flying, and from the birth of our race men have been charmed by it.   *Journal*

✧

We do not ride upon the railroad; it rides upon us.   *Walden*

✧

I fear that I have not got much to say about Canada, not having seen much; what I got by going to Canada was a cold.

"A Yankee in Canada"

WORK AND LEISURE

Let not to get a living be thy trade, but thy sport.   *Walden*

✧

Do not hire a man who does your work for money, but him who does it for love of it.   "Life without Principle"

✧

Unless the human race perspire more than I do, there is no occasion to live by the sweat of their brow.   *Familiar Letters*

There is no more fatal blunderer than he who consumes the greater part of his life getting his living.

"Life without Principle"

✧

Ask me for a certain number of dollars if you will, but do not ask me for my afternoons.   *Journal*

✧

The weapons with which we have gained our most important victories, which should be handed down as heirlooms from father to son, are not the sword and the lance, but the bush-whack, the turf-cutter, the spade, and the bog-hoe, rusted with the blood of many a meadow, and be-grimed with the dust of many a hard-fought field.

"Walking"

✧

The wood-sawyer, through his effort to do his work well, becomes not merely a better wood-sawyer, but measurably a better man.

Familiar Letters

✧

I have seen a man making himself a viol, patiently and fondly paring the thin wood and shaping it, and when I considered the end of the work he was ennobled in my eyes. He was building himself a ship in which to sail to new worlds.   *Journal*

✧

What noble work is plowing, with the broad and solid earth for mater-ial, the ox for fellow-laborer, and the simple but efficient plow for tool! Work that is not done in any shop, in a cramped position, work that tells, that concerns all men, which the sun shines and the rain falls on, and the birds sing over!

Journal

✧

As for the weather, all seasons are pretty much alike to one who is ac-tively at work in the woods.   *Journal*

✧

If I should sell both my forenoons and afternoons to society, as most ap-pear to do, I am sure, that, for me, there would be nothing left worth living for.   "Life without Principle"

✧

There is some of the same fitness in a man's building his own house that there is in a bird's building its own nest.   *Walden*

It is the art of mankind to polish the world, and every one who works is scrubbing in some part. *Familiar Letters*

✧

It is not enough to be industrious; so are the ants. What are you industrious about? *Familiar Letters*

✧

In fact, no work can be shirked. It may be postponed indefinitely, but not infinitely. "Paradise (to Be) Regained"

✧

It is well to find your employment and amusement in simple and homely things. These wear best and yield most. *Journal*

✧

Are we not all wreckers, contriving that some treasure may be washed up on our beach, and we may secure it, and do we not contract the habits of wreckers from the common modes of getting a living? *Journal*

✧

The naturalist accomplishes a great deal by patience, more perhaps than by activity. He must take his position, and then wait and watch. *Journal*

✧

It is a good policy to be stirring about your affairs, for the reward of activity and energy is that if you do not accomplish the object you had professed to yourself, you do accomplish something else. So, in my botanizing or natural history walks, it commonly turns out that, going for one thing, I get another thing. *Journal*

✧

If you have ever done any work with these finest tools, the imagination and fancy and reason, it is a new creation, independent on the world, and a possession forever. You have laid up something against a rainy day. You have to that extent cleared the wilderness. *Journal*